Be a Super Awesome Photographer

LAURENCE KING

Published in 2019 by
Laurence King Publishing Ltd
361–373 City Road
London
EC1V 1LR
United Kingdom
T + 44 (0)20 7841 6900
F + 44 (0)20 7841 6910
enquiries@laurenceking.com
www.laurenceking.com

A catalog record for this book is
available from the British Library.

ISBN: 978-1-78627-420-5

Printed in China

All illustrations by Matt Johnstone

Back cover left:
Elliott Erwitt, *New York City* (1950)
© Elliott Erwitt/Magnum Photos

Back cover right:
Emily Stein, *Bubblegum Boy* (2014)
© Emily Stein

Be a Super Awesome Photographer

Henry Carroll

Laurence King Publishing

Contents

Let's get down to business

This book is the only thing standing between you and photography greatness. Inside, you'll find photos by the world's most SUPER-AWESOME photographers and some equally important "Nifty know-hows" that will help you take next-level pictures!

It's simple. All you need to do is look at the pictures, read a little about what makes them great, and then use your creative skills to take your own photos inspired by these mega-masters!

Some of the challenges you'll find funny and others more serious, some easier and others a little trickier. That's OK, because realizing which challenges you like best, and why, will help you figure out what kind of SUPER-AWESOME photographer you want to be.

You can use any kind of camera, including a grown-up's phone. Just remember to ask first, and please don't drop it, or they'll get super-angry (with you and me). Now turn the page and let's snap to it!

 **Top tips**
Look out for this icon if you need extra inspiration to complete a challenge.

#BeSuperAwesome
Use this hashtag to share your own SUPER-AWESOME photos and to see everyone else's.

Pretend you're a dog

When taking pictures, you should be bending and stretching all the time—a bit like doing yoga. That's what makes this photo by the world-famous photographer Elliott Erwitt so great. Because he lay right down on the ground, his picture shows us a whole different view of the world. In this case, a "dog's-eye view." Poor little pooch— imagine what it must be like walking through the city if everyone's feet look that big! Even the most ordinary subjects look totally different when seen from up high or down low, so try finding your own unusual angles of everyday subjects.

Most people always take pictures from head height, which can be boring because we see the world from that point of view all the time. Imagine how different the world must seem to mice, or even birds —to them everything must seem so big or small!

Elliott Erwitt, *New York City* (1950)

Emily Stein, *Bubblegum Boy* (2014)

Be sneaky

Portrait photographers use all kinds of sneaky tricks to distract the people they're snapping. Look at the picture of this kid by a photographer called Emily Stein. Because Emily made him concentrate so hard on blowing a bubble, he's not paying any attention to the camera. This is way cooler than simply asking someone to say cheese, because you can tell a lot about a person from how they react instinctively to something. Give it a go yourself by photographing people while they're distracted.

You could ask people to hold their breath, jump in the air, or even eat a lime—whatever it takes to make them forget they're being photographed!

See things differently

Most people just see things as they are. When they look at a vacuum cleaner, all they see is a vacuum cleaner. And to them, a pancake is just a pancake. But you know what I see when I look at a vacuum cleaner? A twisting python! And every time I cook pancakes, I see planets! My friend Jesse from Australia is the same. Look at what he saw when he stumbled across this box— a cardboard creature with a friendly face! I bet you have this SUPER-AWESOME power too …

Look for things that appear like something else. You could make the alphabet by photographing objects that look like letters (a steering wheel could look like the letter O), or you could create your own zoo by photographing things that look like animals (maybe a spilt drink looks like a giraffe …).

Jesse Marlow, *Box Face* (2008)

Louis Porter, *Beans* (2005)

Use colorful language

Most people take pictures *in* color, but photographers like Louis Porter take pictures *about* color. That's why this is probably the world's greatest photo of baked beans, a toaster, and a kettle. Look at the amazing colors. The green, orange, blue, and yellow all add up to something way tastier than beans on toast! Explore your local area to find your own SUPER-AWESOME color combinations.

Look for ordinary subjects that catch your eye simply because of their color. Imagine a bright red sign against a blue sky. Or an orange car parked in front of a lush green lawn.

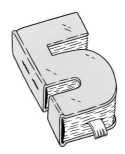

Make up stories

Some photographers, such as Holly Andres, set up or "stage" their photos. What do you think is going on here? Maybe these girls found the key buried in the garden and this is the only lock it fits. I wonder who buried it and if there's a crazy girl-eating granny behind that door! Photos are great in this way, because they're always a bit secretive and never tell us absolutely everything. Try staging photos to get everyone guessing about your own made-up stories.

Think of your picture as a scene from a bigger story. Maybe even write out the whole story and then choose which part to photograph. You could even make a picture that's inspired by your favorite book.

Holly Andres, *Outside the Forbidden Bedroom* (2008)

Composition

To be SUPER-AWESOME at photography, you have to be SUPER-AWESOME at composition. Composition basically means how you choose to arrange or "compose" everything in your photo. Do you place your subject in the middle or to one side? Do you have lots of sky or mostly land? Which way up—vertically or horizontally—do you hold the camera? There's a fair bit to think about when it comes to composition, but to make life easier, here are some handy hacks.

What's your subject?

First, you need to decide on the subject of your photo because photos need to be about something. The subject is the main point of interest in the picture. It could be a person, animal, building, or landscape. It can also be large or small, from a towering skyscraper to a tiny spider.

subject?   subject?

subject?   subject?   subject?

Where are you standing?

You can tell which photographers are SUPER-AWESOME and which aren't just by watching them take pictures. That's because the greatest photographers are constantly moving around trying to find the best angle of their subject, whether it's a landscape, person, or object. Choosing where to take your picture from makes all the difference!

Where do you position your subject in the picture?

Photographers tend to place their subject either in the middle of the picture or to the side. Placing your subject in the middle makes it dominate the composition. Depending on what you're after, this can be a good thing. Placing your subject to one side helps to give a sense of the surroundings.

Nifty know-how: Composition

How do you want the viewer's eyes to move around your picture?

Photographers are always looking out for "leading lines." These guide the viewer's eyes around your composition and lead to the subject. Leading lines can be found everywhere in cities or nature. For instance, roads, rivers, long shadows, and branches make great leading lines. Walk around to see what you can find, then position them in your picture. Look how all these pictures have clear leading lines.

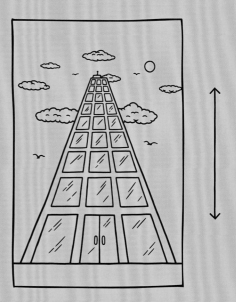

What format?

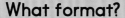

You can hold your camera either vertically or horizontally. Wonky angles aren't cool anymore. Most photographers match the format of their photo to the leading lines. This helps to create a nice natural flow, because horizontal pictures naturally make our eyes move from side to side and vertical pictures naturally make our eyes move up and down.

David Levinthal, *Untitled* from
the series *Wild West* (1987–89)

Make a scene

The photographer David Levinthal uses toy figurines and other props to create mini scenes, which I think is pretty cool. For this photo, he arranged cowboy action figures so that they look like they're having a shoot-out. It's a SUPER-AWESOME photo because we all know that toys are just toys, but David uses them to make the Wild West come to life—yee-hah! Try using toys to create your own scenes.

Get down low when you take your picture so the toys look bigger. Use a lamp to create dramatic lighting and experiment with backgrounds to make the scene look even more theatrical.

Get in shape

Hayley Rheagan takes SUPER-AWESOME pictures of buildings against a bright blue sky. But she doesn't just photograph the whole building. That would be too easy. Instead she only photographs bits of them, which is why they look more like beautiful colored shapes. Photography like this, which reduces the world down to simple shapes, is called "abstract." Practice being abstract around your neighborhood. You can use this technique to photograph anything, not just buildings.

You can make all sorts of objects look abstract by photographing just a section of them, like the curve of a car's hood or the corners of street signs. Don't worry if we can't tell what your pictures are of—that's the whole point!

Hayley Rheagan, from the series *Palm Springs* (2016)

Yasumasa Morimura, *M's Self-Portrait No.56/B*
(or *As Marilyn Monroe*) (1996)

Be self-obsessed

There's this SUPER-AWESOME guy from Japan called Yasumasa Morimura. He loves, and I mean LOVES, dressing up as other people and taking pictures of himself. You wouldn't know it, but this photo shows Yasumasa posing as one of the most famous film stars who ever lived—Marilyn Monroe. It's a strange picture, but also really clever, because Yasumasa does kind of look like Marilyn even though he's Japanese, and a man! Try making a self-portrait while pretending to be someone else. It could be a member of your family or someone famous like Taylor Swift.

Don't just focus on getting the clothes and hair right. Also think about the person's personality, distinctive facial expressions, and body language. Maybe start by recreating an existing photo of them.

Wees smerig

Je zal Maisie Cousins echt heel leuk gaan vinden, want zij is de koningin van smerigheid in fotografie. Soms maakt ze foto's van dingen die ze vindt in het afval. Dat is raar, want je verwacht niet dat afval mooi kan zijn, maar kijk eens naar de manier waarop Maisie de foto gevuld heeft met het onderwerp. We zien meteen alle verschillende kleurencombinaties en texturen. Het ziet eruit als een groot, expressief abstract schilderij! Probeer eens onderwerpen te vinden die normale mensen smerig vinden, en gebruik je fotografie skills om ze van gedachten te laten veranderen. Let er alleen op dat je het niet té gek maakt, want volwassenen houden niet van te veel viezigheid!

Je hoeft niet door het afval te gaan: denk aan de dingen die je in de tuin kan vinden, zoals kleine insecten onder een stuk rottend hout. Denk eraan om de foto te vullen met het onderwerp, zodat de texturen en kleuren eruit springen. Oh, en vergeet niet je handen te wassen voordat je gaat eten!

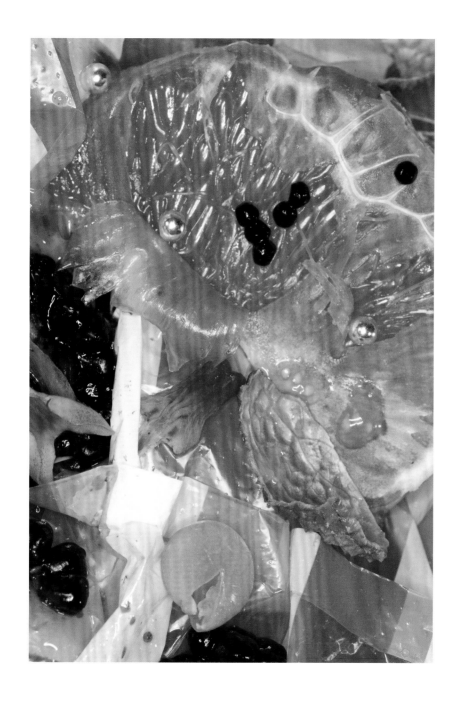

Maisie Cousins, *Rubbish* (2018)

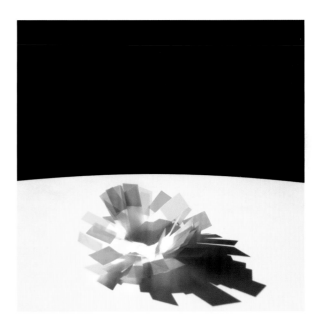

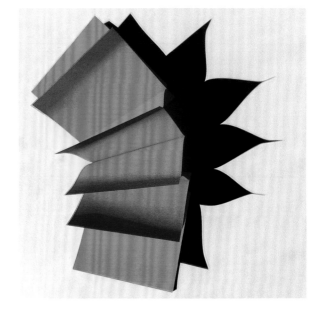

Kathy Ryan, from the series *Office Romance* (2013)

Be hard

Once, when Kathy Ryan was at work, she noticed how the light coming through the windows cast SUPER-AWESOME shadows at certain times of the day. So, Kathy being Kathy, she started exploring with her phone and took photos that transformed the office into a more magical place. I especially like her photos of sticky notes because the shadows make them look like brightly colored exotic flowers. This kind of intense light is called "hard light" (see over the page). For this challenge, take pictures of the strong shadows that fall on different subjects under hard light.

Make sure the sun is out so the shadows are really dark and sharp. Notice how the shadows change the appearance of objects and take this into account when composing your picture. With hard light, it's like the shadows are as solid as the subject itself!

licht

De meeste mensen denken dat licht gewoon
licht is. Maar supergoede fotografen weten
dat er wel meer bij komt kijken. Licht heeft
ontzettend veel persoonlijkheden en het komt
in alle vormen, kleuren en intensiteiten. Hier zijn
slimme tips als het op licht aankomt.

Schaduwen

Schaduwen zijn SUPERCOOL want ze
vertellen ons zoveel over licht. We gaan
eens kijken wat het effect kan zijn bij
een gewone tennisbal...

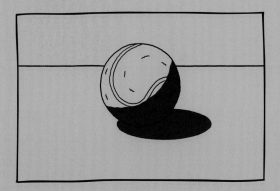

Hard licht

Zacht licht

Schaduwen kunnen donker zijn, met harde randen. Je ziet deze op zonnige dagen, want dan worden ze gemaakt door wat supergoede fotografen 'hard licht' noemen. Hard licht haalt de kleuren naar boven en maakt je foto's superscherp.

Schaduwen kunnen ook lichter met zachte randen zijn. Je ziet deze op bewolkte dagen, want dan worden ze gemaakt door 'zacht licht'. Zacht licht maakt alles een beetje fletser, en de kleuren zijn wat minder aanwezig.

Nifty know-how: Light

Directional light

The harder the light the more "directional" it is, which means it's easier to tell where the light is coming from. This is important when taking photos of people or objects, because it allows you to control where the shadows fall. To ensure the light hits your subject from the best possible angle, you'll often need to reposition the light, the subject, or yourself. See what a big difference the direction of light makes ...

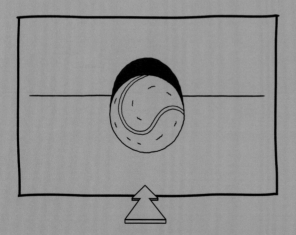

Front light

When something is lit from the front, the shadows are cast behind the subject. This causes a subject to look a bit flat because there are no shadows to give form to the features.

Side light

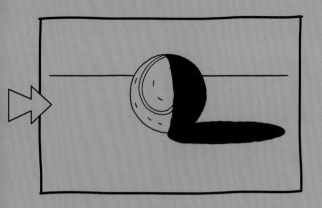

When the light comes from the side, one half of the subject will be bright and the other half dark. This is a nice, classic style of lighting, especially when taking pictures of faces.

Overhead light

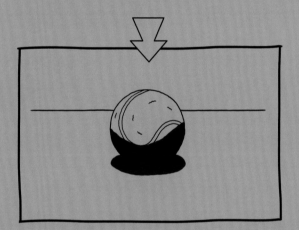

When the light shines on a subject from above, shadows are cast downwards. This can be dramatic, but not so flattering on faces.

Back light

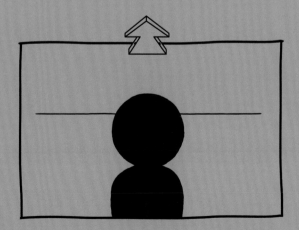

When the light comes from behind the subject, all the shadows are thrown forwards, creating a silhouette. This can look cool, but the shadows will mean you won't see any detail in the subject.

Doe eens wazig

De meeste mensen houden van scherpe foto's. Maar niet deze fotograaf. Yoshinori Mizutani gaat enorm dichtbij bloemen zitten zodat ze voor zijn lens bungelen en prachtige wazige blob-jes worden. Zo krijgt de foto een dromerige sfeer mee, alsof je wakker wordt na een lange slaap en niet precies weet waar je bent. Speel eens met scherpte en wazigheid, zodat je foto's voelen alsof het een oude herinnering of droom is.

Doe wat Yoshinori hier gedaan heeft, en maak eens foto's van een bekende locatie, zoals je huis, school of park. Dit roept dan een gevoel van herkenning op, in plaats van iets totaal onbekends.

Yoshinori Mizutani, van de serie
Voices of Flowers (2016)

Richard Kalvar, *Piazza della Rotonda, Rome* (1980)

Be a joker

This picture by Richard Kalvar cracks me up. First you see the guy in the center and wonder what his friend must be reading aloud to make him look like that. Then you notice the fountain in the background. Now his expression becomes more like "Hey, who's squirting water on my back?!" Of course, the guy isn't really getting wet, but the way Richard has "layered" the foreground (things that are nearer) and background (things that are further away) makes it appear that way. Only SUPER-AWESOME photographers notice things like that. Try layering foreground and background subjects to tell your own joke in a single picture.

It helps to look for your background scene first. Then wait for someone or something to come in front of it to complete the joke. For example, imagine a "no parking" sign with a sleeping dog in front of it … or a billboard featuring a trumpet player behind someone blowing their nose.

Play detective

Look at this picture taken by Larry Sultan, which shows the clutter on his dad's desk. It's SUPER-AWESOME because even though Larry's dad isn't in the photo, we can still get a sense of what type of guy he is just by scanning the objects. He obviously plays golf, he clearly loves dogs, he seems to like bananas if that list is anything to go by, and he's definitely a little disorganized! It's amazing what you can tell about someone by the "evidence" they leave behind. Make portraits of your own family members by photographing the things they leave around.

Think about how tidy or untidy someone is, or notice how they fold a book or what they place on the table as soon as they get home. Habits like these are what make someone individual.

Larry Sultan, *Dad's Desk* from the series *Pictures from Home* (1987)

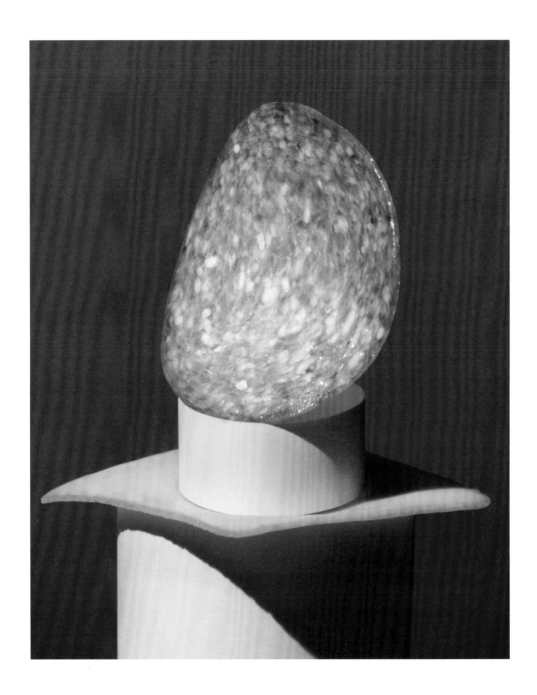

Jiaxi Yang, *Salami Cheese* (2016)

Play with your food

You've probably seen a lot of food photography in cookbooks. But I bet you've never seen photos of food quite like this. The Chinese photographer Jiaxi Yang creates beautiful "still life" photos using familiar foods that we normally just shove in our mouths. See here how Jiaxi has carefully placed and lit this slice of cheese and salami so that it looks like a classical sculpture. Go hunt around the kitchen for interesting-looking foods and make your own still-life photos. Rather than pick foods because they taste nice, think more about what combinations of colors and textures will look best in your photo.

Lighting is super-important when photographing your still life. Think about what direction the light is coming from and whether it's hard or soft. Try setting up your scene near a window or go outside. Turn off your flash, too.

Play tricks

When two young girls, Elsie Wright and Frances Griffiths, took this photo a hundred years ago, they fooled everyone—even the world's brainiest boffins. This is what they did ... First, they cut out pictures of fairies. Then, they went down to the end of the garden, arranged the cut-outs so the fairies looked like they were having a party, and photographed them. Because everyone trusted photos so much back then, they believed that the pictures proved the existence of fairies. Try faking your own photos to see if you can trick the world, too.

Everyone now knows that fairies don't exist, but what about aliens, ghosts, or giants? Use cut-outs and costumes and even think about blurring the picture a little to make it look like you took it on the run. If your photos are convincing enough, you might make front-page news!

Elsie Wright, *Frances with Fairies* (1917)

Cameras

No matter what you're taking pictures with, whether it's a phone or something a bit more posh, think of your camera as just a box with a hole in it. To be a SUPER-AWESOME photographer, you don't need to know everything about how cameras work, but it is helpful to understand a few basics.

How does a digital camera work?

Even though they come in all kinds of different shapes and sizes, a digital camera needs three things to make a photo …

Lens

First, light passes through the lens. This is the glass that you can see on the front of your camera. The job of the lens is to focus light so that your pictures are sharp. SUPER-AWESOME photographers always make sure their lens is nice and clean.

Aperture

After light enters the lens, it passes through a hole called the "aperture." Just like the pupil in your eye, this hole gets bigger or smaller to control the amount of light that passes through. When it's dark, the hole gets bigger so more light passes through. And when it's bright, the hole gets smaller so less light passes through.

Sensor

Lastly, the light hits the sensor. Sensors are magic because they "capture light." When you take a picture in really bright conditions, light hits the sensor for just a fraction of a second. When it's darker, the sensor needs to record the light for a little longer which is why moving objects sometimes look blurry.

More on lenses

Lenses offer you different views of the world. When you look through the camera, some lenses will show you a wide view and make things look further away. These are called "wide angle" lenses.

Other lenses show you a much narrower view and make things look closer. These are called "telephoto" lenses.

Most lenses are "zoom" lenses, which means they allow you to zoom in and out from wide-angle to telephoto, depending on what effect you're after.

Because wide-angle lenses show a wider view, they are good for photographing a big scene. They also make the distance between what's near and far seem greater, meaning details you can easily see with your naked eye might look tiny in your photo.

On the other hand, telephoto lenses show a much narrower view, so they are good for picking out details in a big scene. They also make the distance between what's near and far seem closer, meaning details that might look tiny to your naked eye become really big in your photo.

See how the wide-angle lens captures the "story" of the whole scene and makes things appear far away.

Here the photographer is standing in the same spot but the telephoto lens captures a small detail from the big scene and things in the distance look closer.

Elaine Constantine, *Juliette on Swing* (1998)

Stop time

Harry Potter isn't the only one who can do magic tricks. You can too, because your camera is a magic wand that stops time. Its powers are greatest when you take pictures of moving subjects outside in really bright daylight (I've done it loads of times so you can trust me on that). Look at the girl in this photo taken by fashion photographer Elaine Constantine. You can imagine how fast she was moving, but here she is, frozen in time. Go outside and see if your camera can cast the same spell.

Make sure there's plenty of daylight and then photograph something that's moving. Maybe start by trying to freeze a person jumping or someone throwing balls in the air.

Be wide-eyed

This photo is of the world's greatest boxer, Muhammad Ali. When the photographer Thomas Hoepker took some pictures of him, Muhammad being Muhammad started throwing punches. Look at the size of his fist! Of course, Muhammad's fist wasn't really bigger than his head—that effect is created by the camera's wide-angle lens. When you zoom out and have an object really close to the camera, it makes it look unusually big compared with things further away. Try this out to see if your picture packs a punch.

Start by recreating this photo and then try out the same technique on subjects you find around the house. Remember to place one subject near the camera and the other slightly further away. The closer you get and the more you zoom out, the greater the effect.

Thomas Hoepker, *Chicago, Illinois* (1966)

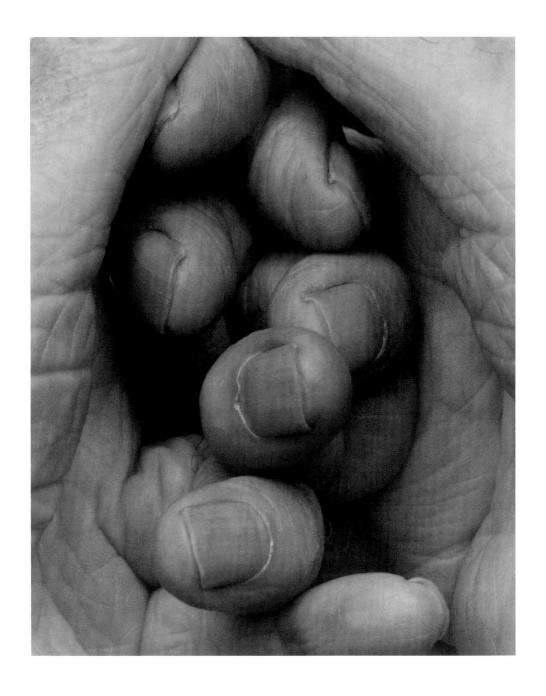

John Coplans, *Self-Portrait, Interlocking Fingers No.16* (2000)

Get closer

There's this artist called John Coplans who likes to do twisty things with his fingers and then take close-up pictures of them. Look at this photo. Because John has photographed his fingers so close up, they start to look a lot less "fingery." Isn't it strange to look at something so familiar and for it to seem so weird? Try taking close-up photos of ordinary things to see if you can make them look strange and unfamiliar.

Fill the frame with the subject, whether that's body parts or other objects you find around the house or garden. Also experiment with black-and-white photos to draw out textures and tones. This helps to make things look less familiar.

Become invisible

When I took this photo, I was invisible. You can tell because no one is looking at me. So how do you become invisible? Easy. First, find a crowded scene where people are busy doing their own thing and aren't paying you any attention. Then, make sure your flash is off, hold your camera by your waist, and take pictures without looking through it. This way, no one sees you taking photos. Try this out next time you're somewhere busy, like a main street or at a friend's party.

This challenge is all about being stealth, so act natural—you're just like any other kid minding their own business. I wonder how close you can get without being noticed ...?

Henry Carroll, *Coney Island* (2013)

Carrie Mae Weems, from the series
Kitchen Table (1990)

Repeat yourself

Sometimes photos work best when they're in a sequence because together they show different aspects of the same subject. This is why Carrie Mae Weems decided to take photographs of herself at her kitchen table. These are just some of the pictures from her series, but see how they show the different roles Carrie has to play at home. She's a mum, a supportive wife, a teacher, and a strong independent woman. It's like she's not just one person, but lots of people. You probably feel that too sometimes. Photograph yourself, a friend, or someone in your family to make a photo-sequence illustrating all their different roles and responsibilities.

Notice how Carrie has kept the location and composition the same in every picture. This is really important in a photo-sequence like this because it creates consistency from one picture to the next.

A snappy history of photography

1826

Joseph Nicéphore Niépce and the oldest surviving photo

The oldest surviving photo was taken by a Frenchman called Joseph Nicéphore Niépce and it shows the view from an upstairs window of his house. Niépce's photo was recorded on a metal plate and was a one-off, meaning it couldn't be reproduced, which was kind of annoying.

1839

William Henry Fox Talbot and the positive/negative process

Englishman William Henry Fox Talbot came up with a photographic process that would later become the most popular. His positive/negative process evolved into camera film which created a negative. This negative was then used to print a positive image like this example of an oak tree. Unlike Niépce's process, this allowed photographers to make loads of copies of the same photo.

The 19th century

Early cameras and photography

Unlike cameras today, early cameras were big, heavy, and hard to use. This meant that early photography was only practiced by professionals, because taking a picture was pretty difficult back then. When taking a shot of nature, photographers often had to bring a whole darkroom with them. And when in the studio, subjects would have to sit very, very still because it could take several minutes to take just one picture!

1900

The Kodak Brownie

In 1900, George Eastman invented a really tasty sounding camera called a "box Brownie." While not actually edible, these Brownies were small, cheap, and easy to use. Eastman also invented a new kind of film that came on a roll meaning it was quick and easy to load. Now everyone, young and old, could take pictures!

A snappy history of photography

The early 20th century

Impromptu pictures

Cameras, lenses, and film gradually became even better meaning you could travel light, take pictures faster, and not be noticed. This allowed photographers like the SUPER-AWESOME Henri Cartier-Bresson to head out onto the streets to capture fleeting moments of everyday subjects. See here how he's caught the man just as his foot is about to touch the water—beautiful!

The 1930s

Color photography

Until now, everyone took photos in black and white, mostly because early experiments with color film looked a bit rubbish. Color photography only started to look better and become more affordable around 1935. But because everyone was so used to black and white, most were a bit snobby about color at first and considered it too "commercial."

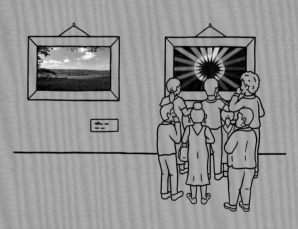

1947

Polaroid pictures

You'll probably find this hard to believe, but until 1947, most people would wait days or weeks to see their pictures because they would send their film off to be developed in a lab. So, when Polaroid instant film was invented, everyone got pretty excited because they could now take photos and watch them develop before their eyes! But Polaroid was expensive and the quality not so good, so most people still preferred good old-fashioned film.

1980s and 1990s

Digital photography

Although digital cameras were invented in the 1970s, it wasn't until the late 1990s that the image quality started to give film a run for its money. People grew to love digital photography because, compared to taking photos on film, it was free and they could see their pictures instantly. So as digital cameras got better and better, fewer and fewer people used film cameras. But even today, some people prefer the magic of film.

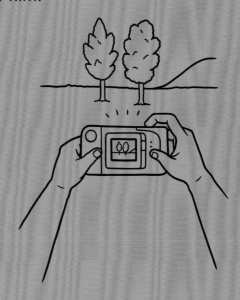

A snappy history of photography

2000

Camera phones

Whoever had the bright idea of combining a camera and a phone changed photography for ever! Almost everyone carries a phone, meaning almost everyone carries a camera, meaning the whole world is now photographed all the time!

2004 – present day

Social media and image sharing

Before the internet and social media, there was no way of instantly sharing a photo with the world. Even news images would take hours or sometimes days to get out into the world. Now anyone can take a photo and post it online within seconds for all to see and share. Kind of cool, but also a bit scary because it means that everything is moving so fast and we end up just "consuming" photographs rather than "appreciating" them.

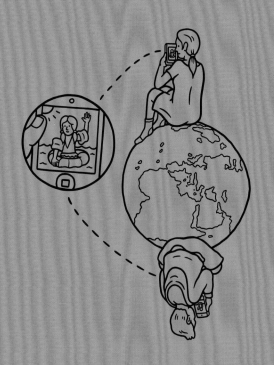

The future

As you can see, photography has come a long way over the last 200 years. I wonder what will happen next? I suppose that's up to SUPER-AWESOME photographers like YOU!

Picture credits

Thanks!

This book would not have been possible without the SUPER-AWESOME help of Melissa Danny, Elizabeth Jenner, Laurence King, Peter Kent, Kate Wiliwinska, Marcela Lopez, Florence Owen, Darcy Owen, and my mum. Special thanks to Matt Johnstone for his brilliant illustrations and to all the photographers who kindly agreed to have their work featured. This book is dedicated to Florence and Darcy. I'm sorry I always forget your birthdays.